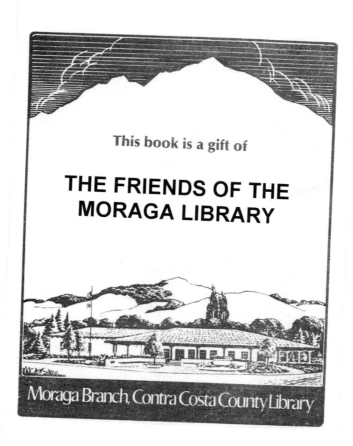

POP CULTURE BIOS
SUPER SINGERS

JUSTIN BIEBER

POP AND R & B IDOL

NADIA HIGGINS

Lerner Publications Company

MINNEAPOLIS

Lerner Publications Company
A division of Lerner Publishing Group, Inc.
241 First Avenue North
Minneapolis, MN 55401 U.S.A.

Website address: www.lernerbooks.com

Library of Congress Cataloging-in-Publication Data

Higgins, Nadia.
    Justin Bieber : pop and R & B idol / by Nadia
Higgins.
      p.   cm. — (Pop culture bios. Super singers)
    Includes index.
    ISBN 978-1-4677-0294-2 (lib. bdg. : alk. paper)
    1. Bieber, Justin, 1994- —Juvenile literature.
  2. Singers—Canada—Biography—Juvenile literature.
  I. Title.
  ML3930.B54A99 2013
  782.42164092—dc23 [B]   2011051068

Manufactured in the United States of America
1 – PP – 7/15/12

Justin's talents are on display at his October 2009 gig at Rockefeller Center.

INTRODUCTION

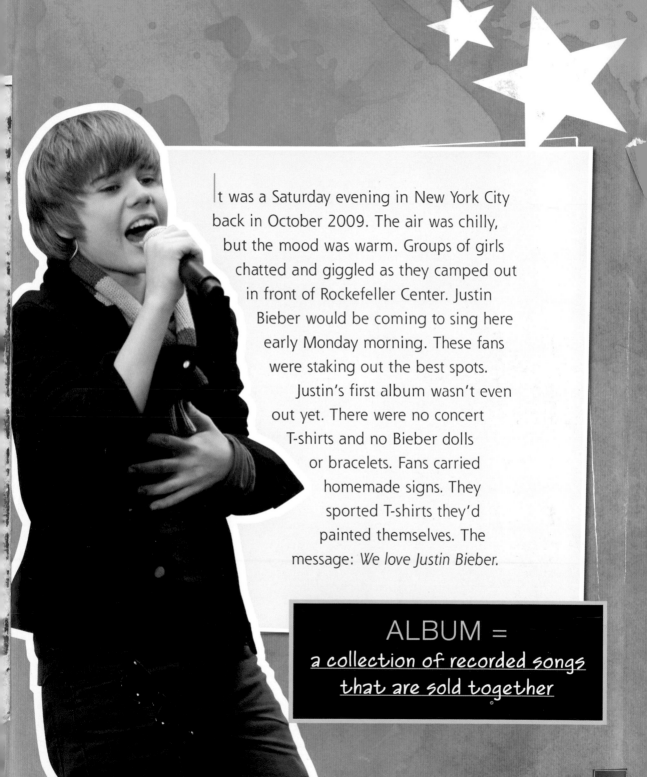

It was a Saturday evening in New York City back in October 2009. The air was chilly, but the mood was warm. Groups of girls chatted and giggled as they camped out in front of Rockefeller Center. Justin Bieber would be coming to sing here early Monday morning. These fans were staking out the best spots.

Justin's first album wasn't even out yet. There were no concert T-shirts and no Bieber dolls or bracelets. Fans carried homemade signs. They sported T-shirts they'd painted themselves. The message: *We love Justin Bieber.*

ALBUM =
<u>a collection of recorded songs that are sold together</u>

Justin couldn't believe fans were already lining up for his Monday gig on the *Today* show. It would be the fifteen-year-old singer's first time on a major U.S. TV network. He wanted to go thank his fans for their support.

The girls were totally stunned when they saw their heartthrob coming their way. Justin signed autographs. Smiling, he put his arms around girls as their cameras flashed and clicked.

By showtime, thousands of fans

AUTOGRAPH = a person's handwritten signature

were crammed around the outdoor stage. Rocking a black jean jacket and a bright purple shirt, Justin performed like a pro. He grooved in time with his backup dancers.

He strummed some sweet guitar. He held his hand over his heart as he hit the high notes.

The whole time, dancing fans jabbed and bumped one another. Girls went hoarse from screaming. Tears streamed down their faces.

Soon, Justin waved good-bye and hurried off to his next event. Nobody could believe how far he'd come. Nobody knew just how far he'd go. But one thing was clear: Bieber fever was on!

screaming fans watch Justin sing his heart out on the Today show.

Aww! What a cutie. These snapshots show Justin as a little guy.

CHAPTER ONE

A NATURAL MUSICIAN

"One-in-a-million chance."** That's how Justin once described his dreams. Not so long ago, he seemed like a pretty average kid. He had a loving family but little money. He had loads of talent but few places to take it.

But Justin also says, "Never say never." He's become more famous faster than any star in the history of pop. He's made it past 15 million followers on Twitter and sold tons of albums. His songs are megahits in at least seventeen countries. How did it all begin?

Hard Times

Justin Drew Bieber was born on March 1, 1994, in the small city of Stratford, Ontario, Canada. His parents, Pattie Mallette and Jeremy Bieber, were only in their late teens when Justin arrived.

When Justin was ten months old, his parents split. His dad moved out of town for work. So Pattie raised Justin as a single mother. Her parents also played a huge role in raising Justin.

Justin grew up as an only child, but his father has since had two children. Justin's sister, Jazmyn, was born in 2008. Little bro, Jaxon, arrived in 2009. Justin says he would do anything for his sibs.

Justin poses with his sis, Jazmyn; dad; and mom in 2011.

Pattie worked hard at several jobs, but as Justin told *Rolling Stone*, times were tight: "I didn't have a real bed. I slept on a blue pull-out couch in my room. We didn't have anything in the fridge, ever, except maybe lunch meat for school, and Kraft macaroni and cheese."

He's Got the Beat

As a toddler, Justin would pound on whatever he could get at. And Justin's pounding had *rhythm*. With help from friends, Pattie managed to get Justin a drum kit when he was four. Justin amazed everybody with his beats.

At the age of five, Justin could hear a song, go to a piano, and figure out the tune in just a few minutes. Pattie knew Justin had a gift, but she didn't have money for music lessons. So she filled Justin's life with music. The radio was always on. Musician friends from church would jam at the house. Justin sang all the time—in the car, in front of the mirror, and even while he brushed his teeth.

JAM =
to play music together

CHURCH PEOPLE

Pattie is a Christian, and she wanted Christianity to be a big part of her son's life. She regularly attended church with Justin. To this day, Justin prays each night before he goes to bed.

With some help from friends and family, Justin taught himself to play the drums, the guitar, and a little bit of trumpet. Music was in his bones. **"I could feel it when the chords and melody didn't fit together the same way you can feel it when your shoes are on the wrong feet,"** Justin would later write.

Fast and Funny

Justin was an active kid. He loved sports, especially hockey. He was smaller than the other players. But he made up for it by being fast and playing smart.

At school, Justin couldn't help being a goofball. He cracked up in class. He drummed on his desk. One time he got sent to the principal. He walked down the hall to the office. Then he just kept on going…all the way to his grandparents' house. They sent him back to school. Justin got grounded when he got home. He used the downtime to practice guitar.

OOH LA LA!

Justin went to a school where everything was taught in French. To this day, he speaks the language fluently.

A Local Star

The year he turned twelve was a big one for Justin. He entered a local singing contest, and he became girl crazy.

FIRST KISS

When Justin was twelve, he set up a dare for his guy friends at a school dance. The first one to kiss a girl would win ten dollars. Only one of them went for it—Justin, of course! "I was slow-dancing with this girl and just went in!" he told *Girls' Life*. "I was lucky she even kissed me back."

(His first crush? Beyoncé.) Justin placed second in the contest. But he totally wowed the audience. He couldn't believe it. Beautiful girls were screaming and cheering *for him*.

That summer, Justin performed outside Stratford's famous Avon Theatre. Tourists coming to see Shakespeare plays found this adorable kid singing his heart out on the stone steps. They'd throw money into his open guitar case. Justin made as much as $200 a day!

Meanwhile, Pattie was posting videos of Justin's performances on YouTube to share with friends and family. The videos started getting hundreds of hits, then thousands. Justin's first fans had found him online. And one of them, Scooter Braun, was about to change Justin's life forever.

A young Justin strums his guitar on the street.

13

CHAPTER TWO

GOT TALENT, WILL TRAVEL

Justin and talent scout Scooter Braun

Scott "Scooter" Braun was actually trying to find another act when he clicked on Justin's video by accident. But the talent scout knew right away he'd found a star.

In the fall of 2007, Pattie and Justin signed a deal with Scooter. He would work to find a recording company interested in cutting Justin's first album.

But breaking into the biz wasn't easy. Justin was only fourteen. The only ways kids his age got to be pop stars was through Disney or Nickelodeon. Nobody had ever become a teen singing sensation through the Internet before.

TALENT SCOUT = a person who finds unknown artists and helps to build their careers

DO U SPEAK BIEBERISH?

Check out these fun expressions used by Justin fans:

- the Biebs = the reason you're holding this book
- Belieber = someone who luvs the Biebs
- non-Belieber = someone who disses Justin; also known as a *hater*
- OMB! = Oh my Bieber! (said, for example, after Justin does a sick drum solo)

Justin and Usher goof around on the red carpet at the Kids' Choice Awards.

Justin needed a mentor, someone to show him what to do—and to prove that he was the real deal. So Scooter arranged for megastar Usher to watch Justin sing. Usher signed on to Team Bieber pretty much right away. And by July 2008, Justin had a deal with a major recording company in Atlanta, Georgia.

The First Hits

By the fall of 2008, Justin and Pattie had moved to Atlanta. Justin's

MENTOR = <u>someone who guides another person in his or her career</u>

next step? Making music. Justin teamed up with a voice coach to perfect his singing. Songwriters came in to create awesome hits. Justin logged long hours in the recording studio. **"[I'd] never worked so hard in my life—and [I'd] never had so much fun,"** he later wrote.

Starting in spring 2009, Justin released four singles, one after the other: "One Time," "One Less Lonely Girl," "Love Me," and "Favorite Girl." The idea was to build excitement for his coming EP—and it worked. All four singles were hits by the time the EP *My World* came out in November. It sold nine hundred thousand copies in five weeks—more than ten times what his recording company had expected. Justin was on fire!

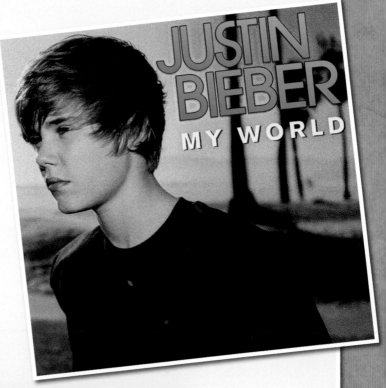

EP =
a recording that is shorter than a full album. *EP* stands for "extended play."

A New Life

With success came huge changes to Justin's life. A typical day for Justin started early in the morning. First up was three hours of studying with a tutor. He no longer had time to attend a regular school. Then he would travel from one event to the next. Everywhere he went, screaming fans and paparazzi greeted him.

Now and then, Justin's BFFs Chaz Somers and Ryan Butler were flown in from Canada to visit. But most of the time, Justin hung with adults. His traveling "wolf pack" included his tutor and voice coach as well as a bodyguard, a publicist (to help with interviews), a stylist (to help with clothes), and Scooter and Pattie.

Sometimes Justin didn't have the chance to just be a kid. Since the early days of Justin's fame, Pattie has been super worried about keeping balance in her son's life. She has always stressed that Justin needs time to chill. To this day, Justin takes a daily nap. He also takes off one day a week to relax. During his downtime, he skateboards, plays Xbox, surfs the Net, and watches sports. And as his friends know all too well, he's always pulling pranks.

Bad Luck (X 2)

Shortly after *My World* came out, Justin learned that fame is not always fun. He was scheduled to appear at a mall in

R u *sure* you want to hang out with Justin? Here are just a few of Justin's past pranks:

- He locked a TV producer in a closet.
- He called up Usher and screamed into the phone like a girl. (He does this a lot.)
- He called Selena Gomez pretending to be her stylist and told her to wear leopard print that day. (She wasn't fooled.)
- He tweeted that his world tour was canceled.

Long Island, New York. As usual, thousands of fans showed up. Then, all of a sudden, people started pushing and shoving. Some fans got knocked down and were stepped on! In the end, five kids had to go to the hospital. And, of course, the event was canceled. Justin felt terrible.

A few weeks later, it was Justin's turn to see the paramedics. He was in London, opening for his friend Taylor Swift. Justin made a wrong step off a ramp and broke his foot—*onstage*. Even though he wanted to scream, Justin kept singing till the end of the song! That night Justin showed how seriously he takes his work.

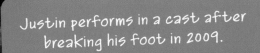

Justin performs in a cast after breaking his foot in 2009.

CHAPTER THREE

IT'S JUSTIN'S WORLD

Justin poses with GF Selena Gomez. What a sweet couple!

- the color purple
- pizza (plain cheese or Hawaiian)
- Band-Aids (He's been known to wear them just for kicks.)
- Rubik's Cubes (He can solve one in less than two minutes.)

Justin's second EP, *My World 2.0*, came out in March 2010. Justin worked with other artists to cowrite all ten songs on this EP. His name appeared in the songwriting credits. He was definitely growing as an artist.

Many people thought it was a risk for Justin to feature rapper Ludacris on the hit "Baby." (Ludacris didn't exactly have a "wholesome" image.) But Justin wanted an edgier sound—and his fans did too. Sales for *My World 2.0* broke all kinds of records. As for "Baby"? A year later, it was the most watched video on YouTube ever, with 500 million hits.

COLD:
THINGS JUSTIN DOESN'T LIKE

- studying
- paparazzi
- elevators (He gets panicky in tight spaces.)
- the dark (He likes a light on to sleep.)

Showtime!

Justin had to get ready for his world tour. He had to work harder on perfecting his hits since his voice was getting deeper. He also had to learn dance moves and set changes. Was he nervous? He says no. He never gets nervous—only psyched—about performing live.

Justin started the North American leg of his My World tour in June 2010. In less than six months, he performed live for two million fans in eighty-five cities. A staff of five hundred people, from dancers to stagehands, made sure that every second of the show was epic.

STAGEHAND =
a worker who is in charge of the set, lights, and props onstage

Tweets are Justin's favorite way to share fan love. Here's one from November 29, 2011: "i promise that i will always b there for you as long as you are there with me. we are a **#FAMILY.**"

All Kindsa Stuff

Meanwhile, Justin was branching out with all kinds of projects. In October 2010, the Biebs became a best-selling author with the release of his autobiography, *First Step 2 Forever: My Story.*

AUTOBIOGRAPHY =
a book about the writer's own life story

Next up was the 3-D documentary *Never Say Never* in February 2011. This blockbuster centers on Justin's My World concert at Madison Square Garden in New York City. A few days before the event, Justin's voice starts to give out from singing so much. (Plus, Justin can't stop talking!) Will the show be called off? This movie shows just how many people are counting on Justin.

That month, Justin also shocked the world with…a haircut. Justin was ready to lose his swoopy do for an older look. Some of Justin's fans were freaked out and even posted hateful comments on the Internet! But Justin didn't care.

GO AWAY, HATERZ

Justin has been the victim of some crazy rumors and other nasty stuff. For a while, there was a rumor that he had died. Once someone hacked into his YouTube videos so viewers were sent to X-rated sites. Justin's take on haters? "U cant bring me down. I wake up everyday grateful 4 the opportunity and grateful to the fans."

Then, in June 2011, Justin launched a perfume that he designed himself. Called Someday, it's been one of Macy's best-selling perfumes ever. Even better? All proceeds go to charity.

Meanwhile, Justin's travel schedule was busier than ever. By November 2011, Justin's My World tour had taken him to six continents. Four years earlier, Justin had never even been on an airplane. Now, he had toured the entire planet!

Justin shows off the perfume he designed.

In May 2011, *Forbes* magazine published a list of the hundred most powerful celebrities. Justin came in at number three. The business mag also spilled how much money Justin had earned the year before: a sweet $54 million.

Jelena

Justin's always said he's totally girl crazy. But for the first time ever, it looked as if Justin was head over heels in love. By fall 2011, "Jelena"—the cosmically cute combo of Justin Bieber and Selena Gomez—was official. Photos of the lock-lipped couple were all over the Net.

With Justin's dream girl by his side, fans got to see just how romantic he could be. One day, Selena mentioned to Justin that she'd love to watch *Titanic* again. So Justin came up with a plan. He rented the Staples Center arena in Los Angeles for a private screening of Selena's favorite movie!

Justin and his sweetie, Selena, hit up the Teen Choice Awards in 2011.

A Bright Future

In November 2011, Justin released *Under the Mistletoe*. The Christmas album topped the charts right away. More important, Justin called it his best album yet. But 2012 saw the release of another album that most fans think is just as awesome—*Believe*. The album features all new hits by the Biebs.

Some people say that, like past teen stars, Justin's fame will die away as quickly as it started. But Justin says no way! He sees himself growing as a musician. He also wants to act in movies. And give more to charity. And spend more time with his family. As Justin told *Vanity Fair*, **"I want to be the best that I can be."**

JUSTIN
PICS!

Justin performs at Disney World's Magic Kingdom in December 2011.

SOURCE NOTES

10   Vanessa Grigoriadis, "The Adventure of Super Boy," *Rolling Stone*, March 3, 2011, http://www .ebscohost.com/ (November 16, 2011).

12   Justin Bieber, *First Step 2 Forever: My Story* (New York: HarperCollins Children's Books, 2010), 56.

13   Daniella Scarola, "Justin Time: First Kiss Confessions. Dream Dates. What He Likes in a Girl. Here's an Exclusive Heart-to-Heart with the Hottest Superstar on the Planet, Justin Bieber. Start. Swooning. Now," *Girls' Life*, February–March 2011, http://www.galegroup.com (November 16, 2011).

16   Justin Bieber, *First Step 2 Forever: My Story*, 163.

23   Justin Bieber, Twitter, posted on November 29, 2011.

24   Justin Bieber, Twitter, posted on April 14, 2010.

27   Lisa Robinson, "The Kid Just Has It," *Vanity Fair*, February 2011, http://www.ebscohost.com (November 16, 2011).

MORE JUSTIN INFO

Bieber, Justin. *First Step 2 Forever: My Story*. New York: HarperCollins Children's Books, 2010. Justin shares his life story in this funny and touching book. It's filled with tons of photos!

BOP & Tiger Beat Online: Justin Bieber
http://www.bopandtigerbeat.com/tag/justin-bieber
Editors of the celebrity mag post tons of updates with the juiciest Justin news. You can also vote in magazine polls and enter Bieber-related contests.

Justin Bieber
http://www.justinbiebermusic.com/default.aspx
Check out Justin's official site to join his fan club, watch videos, and shop for all things Justin.

Justin's Facebook Page
http://www.facebook.com/JustinBieber
Justin keeps you up to date with his latest news. He also posts his favorite videos and interviews.

Nelson, Robin. *Selena Gomez: Pop Star and Actress*. Minneapolis: Lerner Publications Company, 2013. Read all about the other half of Jelena—who's a very talented musician in her own right!

Reyes, Gabrielle. *Justin Bieber: Test Your Super-Fan Status*. Hauppauge, NY: Barron's, 2011. Improve your Bieber IQ through puzzles, quizzes, and fun facts.

INDEX

The images in this book are used with the permission of: © Frederick M. Brown/Getty Images, pp. 2, 24; © Kevin Mazur/WireImage/Getty Images, pp. 3 (top), 14 (bottom right), 23; © George Pimentel/WireImage/Getty Images, pp. 3 (bottom), 10, 28 (bottom left); © Andrew H. Walker/ Getty Images, pp. 4 (top), 7; © Theo Wargo/WireImage/Getty Images, pp. 4 (bottom), 5, 6; Planet Photos/ZUMA Press/Newscom, pp. 8 (top), 8 (bottom left), 8 (bottom right), 9, 11, 13; Mario Anzuoni/REUTERS/Newscom, p. 14 (top); © Charley Gallay/WireImage/Getty Images, p. 14 (bottom left); © Jeff Kravitz/FilmMagic/Getty Images, pp. 16, 29 (top left); AP Photo/PRNewsFoto/ Island Def Jam Music Group, p. 17; © Gerardo Mora/Getty Images, p. 19; © Jason LaVeris/ FilmMagic/Getty Images, p. 20 (top); © Jeff Frank/ZUMA Press/CORBIS, p. 20 (bottom left); © Albert L. Ortega/Getty Images, p. 20 (bottom right); AP Photo/The Virginian-Pilot, Thomas Slusser, p. 22; © Jamie McCarthy/Getty Images, p. 25; © Kevin Mazur/TCA 2011/WireImage/ Getty Images, p. 26; AP Photo/Island, p. 27; AP Photo/Brad Barket/PictureGroup, p. 28 (top left); Splash News/Newscom, p. 28 (right); DP/AAD/starmaxinc.com/Newscom, p. 29 (top middle); © Dwong19/Dreamstime.com, p. 29 (right); Mark Ashman/ABACAUSA.COM/Newscom, p. 29 (bottom left).

Front cover: © Jeff Kravitz/AMA2011/FilmMagic/Getty Images (left); © Steve Granitz/WireImage/ Getty Images (right).
Back cover: © Frederick M. Brown/Getty Images.

Main body text set in Shannon Std Book 12/18.
Typeface provided by Monotype Typography.